LOOM

Kevin Gallagher

MadHat Press
Asheville, North Carolina

MadHat Press
MadHat Incorporated
PO Box 8364, Asheville, NC 28814

The Library of Congress has assigned
this edition a Control Number of
2016908463

ISBN 978-1-941196-32-8 (paperback)

Cover art and design by Marc Vincenz
Book design by MadHat Press

www.madhat-press.com

First Printing

LOOM

List of Illustrations

Table of Contents

for Theo

The Last Lash of the Loom

Antebellum Boston was the "Athens of America" that spawned a new American architecture, the first public hospitals, the dawn of secular music, and the country's first globally renowned poets, writers, and philosophers.

Less known is the fact that the rise of Boston, and the United States as an economic and cultural power in general, was due in no small part to what Massachusetts Senator Charles Sumner called the 'unholy alliance' between the 'lords of the loom' and the 'lords of the lash.'

Eli Whitney's cotton gin enabled Southern plantations to increase cotton production by orders of magnitude. Francis Cabot Lowell's (pirated) importation of the power loom from Manchester, England brought a new era of industrialization to the United States and world economy.

These forces and others triggered unprecedented levels of demand for Southern cotton. In order to make room for cotton slave plantations throughout the South, the Indian Removal Act was passed to relocate Native Americans west of the Mississippi River.

Boston's Lowell, Lawrence, Appleton and other families prospered from this alliance like no other Americans before them and laid the foundation for the United States economy and the Boston we live in today.

Boston's elite admirably re-invested some of their fruits into building a cultured metropolis, but did their utmost to protect their alliance and source of livelihood. Antebellum Boston became a bastion for abolitionist activity but the Boston elites financed counter rallies and periodicals, and the beating of abolitionists on the streets of the city.

This all changed in 1854. Just days after the passage of the Kansas-Nebraska Act—allowing new states to decide whether they would be pro-slavery—escaped slave Anthony Burns was convicted in Boston for violating the Fugitive Slave Act. A riot ensued in the streets of Boston where abolitionists tried to rescue Burns from the Court House. United States Marshalls were brought in to escort Burns and Virginia troops to the Boston Harbor through a riotous crowd of over 50,000 carrying black coffins.

At that moment Amos A. Lawrence said he and other Cotton Whigs became 'stark-mad abolitionists.' Indeed, he himself went on to finance John Brown's efforts to turn Kansas into a free state and to recruit the Massachusetts' 54th 'colored' Infantry. This conversion was pivotal to the course of American history.

This book is inspired by, adapted from, and an echo of numerous speeches, letters, writings, and correspondences of the major players in this drama that still looms overhead today. I sincerely thank Ifeanyi Menkiti, Danielle Legros Georges, Anastasios Kozaitis, Kelly Sims Gallagher, and Fanny Howe for reading and commenting on earlier versions of this manuscript. I also thank the libraries and librarians at the Boston Athenaeum, the Massachusetts Historical Society, the Smithsonian Museum of American Art, the Library of Congress, and the Boston Public Library for preserving and making public their collections. Finally, I thank Marc Vincenz at MadHat Press for his support of and help with this work.

The tale of how we suffer, and how we are delighted, and how we may triumph is never new, it always must be heard."
—JAMES BALDWIN

It's when we face for a moment
the worst our kind can do, and shudder to know
the taint in our own selves, that awe
cracks the mind's shell and enters the heart
—DENISE LEVERTOV

He wants to have the feet of his understanding on the ground, his ground, the only ground that he knows, that which is under his feet.
—WILLIAM CARLOS WILLIAMS

I
UNHOLY ALLIANCE

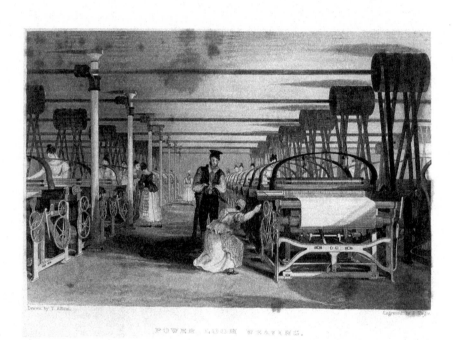

Figure 1. *Power loom weaving.*

Pirating the Power Loom

Francis Cabot Lowell to Nathan Appleton, 1813

I stole their designs with my own two eyes.
I smuggled them to Boston in my mind.

Exporting designs meant jail in Britain.
Workers of looms weren't allowed to leave.

So I snuck into Manchester myself.
I made it back two days before the war.

I saw iron cards and spinning jennys!
I watched Luddites spin and weave all alone

while the looms marched in teams and didn't rest.
I said to myself *this has to come home.*

My baggage was searched twice at Halifax.
They didn't find drawings of their machines.

I sketched it all out in my memory!
I had their designs in my head with me.

Girl Power

Francis Cabot Lowell to Paul Moody, 1813

I teamed up with my old friend Henry Lee.
We put 8,000 dollars down

for cotton plantations in South Carolina.
We saw the money in the cotton gin.

We see even more in our new machines.
With the war the South has nowhere else to go.

Against next year's crops we'll give them loans.
Our ships will sail the cotton up the coast.

Our railroad will roll cotton to the mills.
Our rivers will make the waterwheels go.

Our country girls will man all the looms
and turn cotton to cloth under one roof.

The girls will feel too fortunate to strike.
When wheels roll, spindles whirl, and shuttles fly!

Moody's Miracle

The raw cotton passes through the willow.
The scutching and the spreading machines

separate, clean, and spread the cotton clouds.
Then off the cotton goes to the carding mill.

Fibers get combed and fleeced in a sliver.
The sliver fits into a dressing frame.

The rolling frame makes the coarse and loose thread.
The throstle (or mule) is there to spin the yarn.

The dining machine flips the twist from cops
onto bobbins, then to the warping mill.

The warp is dressed and wound on weaving frames.
The cotton thread is then ready for the loom.

One girl can attend to two looms at once.
She learns this business in about a month.

Tariff Act

Thomas Jefferson, 1816

Small farms
and small squares,

scores and scores
across each state.

Our land, our gardens,
our crops, our fare,

by craft, by hand,
by mule and genteel slaves

is what I see
as our nation's fate.

I am not a Hamilton man
in a rage

but just this time
the plantation and loom

need to be behind
the same wall.

Anyone opposed
wants to reduce us

to a dependence
on that foreign crown

and clothe us in skins
to live like wild clowns

in dens and caverns.
For this, I turn around.

Removal Act

1830

I.

Maize, beans, squash—
the three sisters.

Rabbit, deer, fish,
pots, baskets, clothes.

Trade you skins and fur—
otter, lynx, fox—

for knives, axes, muskets,
gunpowder and scarlet ribbon.

II.

We need
unused lands.

Master the arts
of civilization

or go west
of the Mississippi.

III.

Alabama,
half of Georgia,

western Tennessee.
The Creeks,

Cherokee, Chickasaws.
A trail.

IV.

Horses and oxen
standing up

in the mud
stiff and bones.

One wagon
for every fifty—

for children
for elders

for the rest of us
on foot in tears.

Bayonets at our backs,
disease ahead.

V.

Destined to perpetuate
our race,

to attest
the humanity

and justice
of these states.

Figure 2. Pictorial Life of Andrew Jackson

Breeding Negroes

from Olmstead

I.

As much attention is paid
to the breeding

of Negroes
as to horses and mules.

We raise them both
for the market.

Planters command their girls
and women—

married or not—
to have children.

I have known
a great many Negro

girls to be sold
for having no children.

II.

There's a cotton nigger
for you!

Genuine! Look at his toes!
Look at his fingers!

There's a pair
of legs for you!

He's just as good
at ten bales

as I am for a julep
at eleven o'clock!

If you have not
the right yield

and divine overseer
buy him

and put your faith
in Providence!

These are field-chattels that made cotton king,
(Tho'call'd by loyalists no such thing)
That lay in the house that Jeff built.

Figure 3. *The House that Jeff Built*

The Lowest Class

There was just two classes
to the white folks—

buckra slave owners
and poor white folks

that didn't own no slaves.
There was more classes

amongst the slaves.
The first class was

the house servants.
Then was the butler,

the maids, the nurses,
chambermaids, and cooks.

The next class was
the carriage drivers

the gardeners,
the carpenters, the barber,

and the stable men.
Then come the next class

the wheelwright, wagoners,
blacksmith, slave foreman.

The next class I 'members
was the cow men

and the niggers
that care for the dogs.

All these have good houses—
never git a beatin.

Then come the cradlers
of the wheat, the threshers.

Then come the feeders
of the cotton gin.

The lowest class,
cotton field niggers.

Figure 4. New England Factory Life

Lowell, Massachusetts

1812

'A river ran
green farm lands
lay beyond

And forests
dark against the dreamy hills.

A river less
Romantic than the Rhine

yet fringed
with unwritten histories.'

100 acres,
2500 people.

$15/acre?
Sold!

1850

       34 cotton mills
  7,524 mill girls
  2,427 mill males
 19,376 power looms
305,004 spindles
 38,000 people
     45 schools
     22 churches
800,000 pounds of cotton each week
100,000 pounds of wool each week

Lowell Cloth

Negroes should be
permitted to dress

only in coarse stuffs
such as coarse woolens

or worsted stuffs
during the harsh winter.

Coarse cotton stuffs,
felt hats and coarse

cotton handkerchiefs
for summer—

all made by girls
and invisible men

in fields in mills
who know rivers

from the Nile
to the Merrimack.

Lucy Larcom

I ask you how much of your wrong is mine
as I change bobbins in the spinning room.
As the waters glide and our shuttles fly

you toil in ghastly death-sown fields that lie.
All day I stand before a power loom.
I ask you how much of your wrong is mine

down underneath the 'tearless Southern sky'?
My family needs me to send money home.
As the waters glide and our shuttles fly

it isn't very hard to draw straight lines.
I work here five years then find a groom.
I ask you how much of your wrong is mine.

I cannot weave when I'm wearing blinds.
I'm not alone because I am with you.
As the waters glide and the shuttles fly,

clasp my hands and look right in my eyes.
You will see the sun of the Southern sky.

As my shuttle flies and the water glides
I ask you how much of your wrong is mine.

Athens of America

Abbott Lawrence, 1830

I.

I'm not convinced war is to be so loathed.
The British couldn't sell their cloth over here.

Merchants had nowhere to go but the coasts.
Banks could no longer invest over there.

So we sent ships to the Carolinas
and brought the cotton straight to Boston.

My brother married Nancy Means Ellis,
Robert Means of South Carolina's cousin.

We made fortunes with Lowell in Waltham.
We made our own towns, Lawrence and Lowell.

A Lowell married my daughter Katherine.
My nephew married an Appleton.

Office on State Street, house on Beacon Hill.
I go to the same church as Nathan Hale.

II.

Attending Brattle Square Church in Boston,
we sit back in our pews every Sunday—

the best diagonal line that can be drawn
from Jesus to Abbott Lawrence, so they say.

For the week I wake and walk down Beacon Hill.
I sit in my good office on State Street.

I prepare correspondence by my windowsill.
I survey accounts and look out at the fleet

of ships that brings goods in and sends mine out.
At noon I gather my hat and my stick.

I then take a mid-day walk about town.
I meet my associates at Topliffs.

We discuss weather, trade, and the ports.
I wear a swallow-tail coat, calfskin boots.

III.

For Gottlieb Graupner

Music in a church serves a great purpose
but language and text only go so far.

Close your eyes and feel the hymodic force.
History is good, but now we have time

to go out and see over the steeples
to hear and feel what holds and makes us move

to bring the music to all the people
no matter where they go on their Sundays.

Beethoven is higher than cathedrals,
Handel and Haydn are more than the Messiah.

The force of nature could no further go,
I don blackface and bring minstrel songs.

The music has spread all over the world.
We open our mouths and bring a new choir.

IV.

Jim Crow Minstrel

I went down to New Orleans
feeling so full of light—

even though they threw me in a calaboose
and locked me inside all night.

When I got out I hit a man.
Don't ask me his name, I forgot.

But there was nothing left of him
but a little speck of a grease spot.

And the other day I hit a man.
I must say the guy was mighty fat.

I hit him so hard that I
knocked him into an old cocked hat.

I kneel to the buzzard, bow to the crow,
Every time I wheel about I jump just so.

INTERIOR VIEW OF S. KLOUS & CO.'S HAT, CAP AND FUR STORE, NO'S 29 AND 31 COURT STREET, BOSTON.

Figure 5. Gleason's; S. Klous & Co. Hat, Cap, and Fur Store, Court Street, Boston

City Upon a Hill

Minds as active as our hands.
We are congenial gentleman.

Here the dollar sinks amidst better gods.
We trust our cotton as we trust our cod.

We know what we are doing with our wealth.
Bulfinch builds our 'City Upon a Hill.'

Hospitals, libraries, our asylums.
Observatories and athenaeums.

The Dial, Atlantic Monthly, Observer—
but not a cent for *The Liberator.*

Done with the courtly muses of Europe.
Done with the old antique and future worlds.

Led by the wise, the well-born, and the good.
We will make sure this place is understood.

Goodwill Tour—The Prince's Diaries

Amos A. Lawrence, 1835

Kentucky

The stationer's shop was well stocked
with pistols, bowie knives, and tobacco.

Perhaps he sold some books and some paper.
But this is Kentucky, I do not know.

I went looking for a church on Sunday.
I found men reading Bibles in cabins.

Grocery shops were open. Drunks plodded about.
I saw two men lying down in the street.

I saw two fights on the very same day.
I saw two more fellows get stuck with knives.

I wonder what they do on the weekdays.
I wonder what they say to their wives.

I'm finding it very different here.
Shake all their hands and try not to stare.

Georgia

The want of thrift among the farmers
is far and beyond what I can understand.

This must arise from their ignorance.
Their lack of erudition, and attention.

Consequently their want of facility
of information lasts all day and night.

The countryside is very beautiful.
The ladies are pretty and polite.

What I had imagined as the Southern
planter is an exceedingly rare sight.

Some days when it is hot as hell
every man is burning for a fight.

I am finding it very different here.
Shake hands and try not to stare.

LOOM

Alabama

I believe a Negro child never cries
except those fallen into sleep.

Here comes a covered cart drawn by mules.
I see the floating eyes that peep—

wooly heads of a dozen Negroes laughing.
I believe a Negro child never cries.

Grown Negroes hunt squirrels in the woods.
Those processions can become quite ragged

but the Negroes dressed with warm little hoods.
I believe a Negro child never cries.

I believe Negro adults never lie.
Sometimes they seem pretty much as equals.

In my mind this is deservedly so
for they seem to know about as much.

Virginia

The Negroes in the country seem healthy,
happy, and are always respectful here.

A planter passing a Negro will nod,
bid him good day, or ask of his master.

If they are well-bred and see a carriage
some Negroes touch their hats or take them off.

The condition here appears to be much better.
The planters here who know about Boston

say they feel under great obligation
to my uncle Mr. Abbott Lawrence

who was quite civil to them in his home town.
They attended a party at his house.

We may never see eye to eye
but let us look in the same direction.

II
POLIS WAS THIS

Turnout

Harriet Hanson Robinson

When the cotton is all spun
and all our work is done,

the boss man takes the money
and we get close to none.

Now they want to cut our wages,
make us pay our own board.

We have to show our faces
in the name of our Lord.

I know what I have to do.
I am going to turn out.

I ask that you will join me too,
march with me and shout:

'Oh isn't it a pity
such a pretty girl as I

should be sent to the factory
to pine away and die.

Oh I cannot be a slave
For I am so fond of liberty

That I cannot be a slave!'
No, I cannot be a slave.

Warning Shots

John Floyd, 1831

I lay Nat Turner
on Boston's doorstep.

Militias now swarm
my entire state.

We killed one hundred
and hunt for more.

All of our planters
are watching their backs.

You must take action
or we'll kill more blacks.

We pin the blame
on *The Liberator*—

a diabolical
Boston paper

edited by a madman
at your Merchant's Hall!

There is too much excitement
across the whole South

of this illegal notion
you call abolition.

The Lowell turnout
does not help.

Your Lowell girls sing,
or so we are told,

'I'm so fond of liberty.
I cannot be a slave!"

Prepare for some harsh
resolutions toward

your manufactures, friends.
You people up North

must go to hanging
those fanatical wretches

if you would not lose
your Southern trade.

Letter of Reassurance

Harrison Gray Otis, 1832

We will never support abolition
unless requested by our brethren,

our partners in wealth, our slave-holding states.
We don't doubt that the States in this Union

are inhibited by a federal compact
from interfering with the plantations

in the management of their own slaves.
We promise to keep this Union intact.

Slavery exists by the constitution.
It is your sovereign right to make a choice.

Many here have chosen to colonize them.
That means nothing but money for your boys.

You and I may never see eye to eye
but let us look in the same direction.

Colonization

Amos A. Lawrence, 1833

The greatest change in the life of blacks
than any time since the Christian era!

They'll never be truly free North or South.
It is thus better to ship them out.

A good-looking black preacher came to ask
for money to free his family

of eleven and sail for Liberia,
to be free and gone once and for all

even if they could move on to free soil.
He had just learned his daughter had died.

I found many tears come from my own eyes.
I gave six thousand dollars for his ride.

He took my hand as he went out, saying
you are the friend for which I've been praying.

Figure 6. *The cradle of liberty, interior, Faneuil Hall, Boston—scene of epoch-making meetings of two centuries*

Faneuil Hall

Harrison Gray Otis, August 21, 1835

The thirteen stripes and a square of stars
can't become dismal strains of black and red.

The maniacs call our constitution
a covenant with death, agreement with hell,

and unfathomably deep with pollution.
They do not work like Christian gentleman.

They preach for the repeal of our Union.
I warn them of the danger of their meeting.

They ask for appeal to a 'higher law'.
This is war in disguise upon our lives;

a war on property and faith of contract,
an outrage upon our pride and honor.

We will never see eye to eye.
Stop them from going in that direction!

Figure 7. *Ladies Department,* The Liberator. *William Lloyd Garrison, editor*

Female Anti-Slavery Society

Mayor Lyman vs. Mary Parker, October 21, 1835

Go home, ladies. Go home. You must go home.
Go home. This is a crime that can't be atoned.

What renders it why we should go home?
We are just meeting. We have done nothing wrong.

Ladies, do you wish to see bloodshed here?
If you do not I want you to go home.

Your personal friends instigate this mob.
Why can't you use your influence with them?

I am merely a public official.
Ladies, you must retire. This is dangerous.

If this is the last bulwark of freedom
we may as well die here as anywhere.

Go home, ladies. Go home. You must go home.
Go home. This is a crime that can't be atoned.

Figure 8. *Masthead,* The Liberator, *William Lloyd Garrison, editor*

The Liberator

William Lloyd Garrison, 1835

Thousands of genteel ruffians called out:
Lynch him! Lynch him! Hang him in the Common!

Turn him a right niggar color with tar!
I ran and jumped out of the back window

only to land on an even larger mob.
The Cooley brothers pinned both my shoulders

then lashed a rope three times around my chest.
I was dragged through Wilson's Lane to State Street

to the spot of the Boston Massacre.
They tore off my clothes and kicked my face.

The light of day did not cause them to care,
so the Mayor jailed me to keep me safe.

Another day devoted to Thy cause.
Not till war is over will I pause.

This Is No Party

Wendell Phillips, 1835

Gentleman of broadcloth in broad daylight
came from State to Washington Street a mob.
You dragged a man through Boston without right.

These were his unalienable rights.
Your mob wasn't workingmen or rabble
but Brahmins in broadcloth in broad daylight.

It was all too clear what was in their sight.
You surrounded him to pummel and rob.
You dragged him through the streets without his rights.

Never before had I seen such a sight.
Never so hard had both my eyes sobbed.
Gentleman in broadcloth in broad daylight,

you pride yourselves on the prayers you say each night
but deny to protect your precious cloth.
You dragged a man through Boston without right.

I stand by him. From now on I fight
until every trace of slavery is gone.

You dragged a man through Boston without right.
Gentleman of broadcloth in broad daylight.

The Boston Whig

Everywhere outside of New England
we are heartily despised for all this

greediness for all gain, this selfishness
of the manufacturing interest

now so identified with all we Whigs.
We hereby protest against this Union.

We are capable of higher, nobler
purposes than the worship of Mammon.

Monopoly by manufacturers
is a monopoly of the worst sort.

Yours is an abstract principle of right,
wholly unworthy of the Pilgrim race.

You have planter's whip-poppers in your buttonholes.
Your heads are pillowed on cotton unsold.

The Cotton Whigs

Abbott Lawrence, 1845

I.

It's easy to be a man of conscience
if you don't have anything to lose.

I favor maintaining our compact.
I'm in support of the Union as is.

I do not have an ounce of sympathy
for the mischief of abolitionists

who threaten freedom in several states.
The emancipation of all the slaves

has been and will be delayed by the wild
efforts of radical minorities.

The abolition of slavery in
these states will always be a State question.

I do not feel that I should meddle
or interfere in any shape or form.

II.

You are just trying to get back on top.
You feel like you have lost the position

that you used to have in our Commonwealth.
It is not that you really like Garrison.

I don't want slaves any more than you do.
On God's earth they are a complete disgrace.

We have to hold the Union together.
The Constitution says they can have their slaves.

That is why Garrison calls it a
'covenant with death, agreement with hell'

but the solution is not to secede.
Forget Old North Church, the Liberty Bell?

How can you be taking him seriously?
We all lose unless we have unity.

III.

We would say good-bye to every loom.
How could I look in the eyes of my bride?

Our merchants now live or die by the coast.
Your job depends on South Carolina.

No more Handel and Haydn Society.
We would go back to wearing British cloth.

No support for Horace Mann and his schools.
The Lowell girls will go back to mother.

Democrats aren't going to free the slaves.
All of this is going to take some time.

Do you really want to hand them the keys?
Separate your heart from your mind.

Remember what John Quincy Adams said:
'our fighting keeps a crown on Jackson's head.'

Compromise of 1850

Cotton thread binds the Union together.
Each one of us wears the same wig.

We sign a stronger Fugitive Slave Act.
California comes in as a free state.

Popular sovereignty for Utah
and New Mexico. Ten million dollars

paid to the slave state of Texas,
but no more slaves in Washington, DC.

This will prevent a blockade from the South
and further retreat over to Free Soil.

Bound in honor to preserve the compact.
Bound also to prevent the spread of slaves.

You and I may never see eye to eye,
but let us look in the same direction.

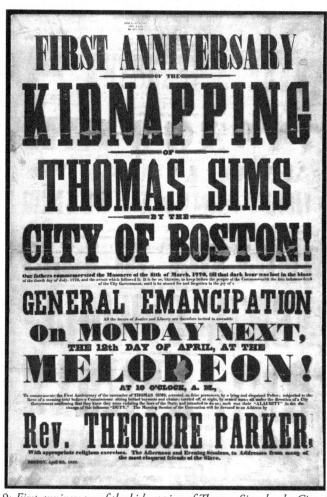

Figure 9: *First anniversary of the kidnapping of Thomas Sims by the City of Boston*

Thomas Sims

to the Boston Committee for Vigilance and Safety, 1851

As I was stabbing everyone I could
I screamed 'I'm in the hands of kidnappers!'

Slave hunters snuck up behind my back.
I had no time to even think to run.

I will not be allowed to speak in court.
I go back if they prove I was a slave!

Edward Barnette said he saw me when I
dressed as a sailor at a blow-out ball,

and that is all it takes to send me South.
Southern planters possess some wizard art

unknown to the demons of former times.
You ask me to jump out of my window

and join the airy whirl of the free world.
Let the heavens weep and hell be merry!

Sold Down River

John Pearson, owner of the Gilmore

The *Gilmore* runs cotton to Boston
then brings the cash back to Savannah.

So I paid for one hundred and fifty men
to stand in a hollow box at Court Square

near police that had swords on their shoulders.
Each one of mine had a club or a hook.

We grabbed Sims and marched him in the middle—
through the crowds to board at Long Wharf.

We sent Sims straight to the Chatham Country Jail
where he got thirty-nine stripes of the lash.

I raise my glass to the North and the South!
May the links of our chain bind very strong!

May abolitionists be pitched to hell!
May Bunker Hill be rolled against the gate!

Era of Good Feelings

I fervently hope the question will rest
and that no sectional or ambitious

or fanatical excitement will test
the durability of our institutions

or obscure the light of prosperity.
Sterling intelligence, integrity,

and the patriotism of the people
will prevent suicidal madness and be free

of talk of secession or disunion.
We should never wake the sleeping tiger

who would bring these states back to ruin.
In his sleep he growls when he is stirred.

We shall now bring this matter to a close.
We are in a state of perfect repose.

III
STARK-MAD ABOLITIONIST

Figure 10. *Portrait of Anthony Burns*

Anthony Burns

Boston, May 24, 1854

I didn't want to make myself known.
I didn't tell who I was.
I got employed.
I came to work.
I worked hard.
I kept my own counsel.
I strove for myself.
I didn't say I was a slave.

I was going home.
I heard someone behind me.
I felt a hand on my shoulder.

I heard the cannons.
I think from the Common.
I hear because the Nebraska bill just passed.

'Stop, stop, you are the fellow
that broke into the silversmith's shop!'

I said he was mistaken.
I was lifted off my feet.
I think by six or seven others.
I could not resist.
I could not speak.

I waited in the courthouse.
I waited for some time.
I said I wanted to go home.
I said I wanted my supper.
I waited in the jail.

'How do you do, Mr. Burns?'
said the man who opened the door.

I said
I am fine, my Master.

'Did I ever whip you, Anthony?'
I said No.

'Did I not when you were sick
take my bed from my own house for you?'
I said Yes.

'Did you ever ask me for money
when it was not given to you?'
I said I do recollect.
You gave me twelve and a half cents
At the end of every year.

I was taken down
with bracelets on my wrists.
Not such as you wear ladies,
of gold and silver.

I was taken down
with bracelets on my wrists.
Iron and steel manacles
that wore into my bone.

Handbill

Boston Vigilance Committee, May 25, 1854

CITIZENS
OF
BOSTON

A free citizen of Massachusetts—
Free by Massachusetts Laws until His Liberty is Declared to be
Forfeited by a Massachusetts Jury, is

NOW IMPRISONED

In a MASSACHUSETTS
TEMPLE OF JUSTICE!

The compromises trampled on by the SLAVE POWER when in the
path of Slavery, are to be crammed down the throat of the North!

THE KIDNAPPERS ARE HERE

Men of Boston! Sons of Otis, and Hancock,
and the "Brace of the Adamses!"

See to it that Massachusetts Laws are not outraged with your
consent! See to it that no Free Citizen of Massachusetts is dragged
into Slavery

WITHOUT TRIAL BY JURY '76

NIGHT ATTACK ON THE COURT HOUSE.

Figure 11. *Night Attack on the Court House*

Rescue Attempt

Thomas Wentworth Higginson, May 27, 1854

There is now no law in Massachusetts.
When law ceases we act in sovereignty.

We rushed State Street like the sweep of wave.
We started breaking out the battle axes

and a battering ram for the front door.
We threw brickbats to break the windows.

The guards started shooting at us from above.
Surrounding crowds screamed 'Take him out! Rescue him!'

Muzzles flashed and pistols cracked behind us.
We pounded inside and started stabbing.

We killed an Irishman of the Marshall's guard.
They clubbed us back on the street with the crowds.

Their cutlasses proved too much for us.
Cowards! Would you desert us now?

Figure 12. *The rendition of Anthony Burns in Boston*

The Stark-Mad Abolitionist

Amos A. Lawrence, May 25, 1854

I put my hands in my face and I wept.
I went to bed an old-fashioned conservative,
I woke up a stark-mad abolitionist.

Look what you've done. I can do nothing less.
You've given me a new purpose to live.
I put my hands in my face and I wept,

then I put myself into his footsteps.
Burns is a hero, not a fugitive.
I am a stark-mad abolitionist.

I will see to it that we free Kansas.
Your betrayal is my strongest motive.
I put my hands in my face and I wept

but woke up a new man after I slept.
I will give everything I can give.
I am a stark-mad abolitionist.

Anthony Burns I will never forget.
Stephen Douglass I will never forgive.

I put my hands in my face and I wept.
Now I'm a stark-mad abolitionist.

Skunk Peculiarities

Richard Henry Dana, May 26, 1854

I found Amos A. Lawrence at my door,
a man who has long appeased Slave Power.

He said he wanted to go on record
that he changed his mind in the final hour.

The man who gave help to arrest Shadrach.
The man who paid to send back Thomas Sims.

The man whose textile girls say they are slaves.
The man whose mob may have dragged Garrison

told me he will spend whatever it takes
to help to defend this fugitive slave.

Nebraska and Burns were too much to take.
'We're no runaway hunting ground!' he said.

Now we have the 'solid men' of Boston
on our side and on the side of freedom!

Escort

153   men and guns
1st Battalion Light Dragoons
under Major T.J. Pierce

339   men and guns
5th Regimen of Artillery
under Colonel Robert Cowdin

280   men and guns
5th Regimen Light Infantry
under Colonel Charles Holbrook

112   men and guns
3d Battalion Light Infantry
under Major Robert I. Burbank

80   men and guns
Divisional Corps of Independent Cadets
under Lt. Colonel Thomas C. Army

125   men and guns
Columbian Artillery
under Captain Thomas Cass

n.a.   men and guns
U.S. Marines
under Major S.C. Ridgely

The Foot of Slave Power

Samuel May Jr., June 2, 1854

A body of troop with drawn swords
and a large force of police and marines

surrounded a hollow square
hemmed by a thick-set hedge of gleaming blades

and large brass field-piece with artillery—
loaded to the muzzle and more than ready.

In the midst of this walked Anthony Burns.
Fifty thousand rushed in all around them.

Fifty thousand carrying black coffins.
Companies of mounted horsemen rushed on,

dividing and scattering us for a time.
He has gone off to their tender mercies.

He has gone! Boston lies bound hand and foot!
Slaves at the foot of Slave Power!

The Blood of '76

Amos A. Lawrence, 1854

Three years ago I offered my support
to protect U.S. Marshals from the mob.

This time I prefer to see the court razed
than see this man's freedom robbed.

They marched him down State Street in procession.
Cavalry, artillery, and heavy cannon.

U.S. troops before him and behind.
He held his head up and marched like a man.

The windows on houses were filled with faces,
though the streets and alleys had all been cleared.

We thought Boston the safest of places,
that here freedom could never disappear.

We cannot stand that this was not a crime.
I have to tell you that it is high time.

Not Now as a Servant, but Above a Servant

Anthony Burns

I admit
I left my master
I refused to return

I deny
I disobeyed the law or God

I was stolen
I was made a slave as soon as
I was born

His man-stealing gave him no right to me
God made me a man not a slave
God gave me the same right to myself that
God have the man who stole me to himself

You charge that
I disobeyed God's law?
No, indeed!

God wrote his law on the table of my heart
God makes me love freedom
God's good hand in mine

I walked out of the house of bondage

but, if thou may be made free, use it rather
thou shalt not deliver unto his master the servant
which is escaped from his master unto thee

He shall dwell with thee
even among you in that place
which he shall choose
in one of thy gates
where it liketh him best
thou shalt not oppress him

I was stolen

He that steals a man and sells him
or if he be found in his hand

He shall surely be put to death

AMOS A. LAWRENCE
of Boston, Founder of L. University.

Figure 13. *Amos A. Lawrence of Boston.*

Unwound

Amos A. Lawrence, June 1854

You have defied me twice in the same day.
I unwind all my positions with you.

I kiss their hands then wave good-bye to your ladies.
Your cotton will not be used in my looms.

Our money will not be loaned to you or paid.
You came up here and all hell broke loose.

Shame shame shame that Anthony Burns parade!
Kansas and Burns crossed the line we drew.

Now it is time to free all the new states.
I know that I have so much more to lose

but there's more to this than what I have *made*.
There is no other course that I can choose.

I cannot go any further with you.
I know what it is I that I have to do.

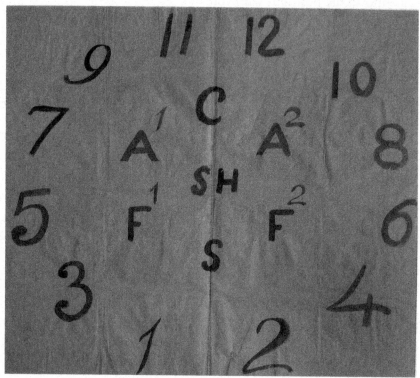

Figure 14. *Diagram to show the drill the Anti-Man-Hunting League had for the running off of a slave- or man-hunter*

Boston Anti-Man-Hunting League

Henry I. Bowditch, 1854

A committee of six: prudent, young, true,
and stalwart comrades—with one elder

speaker—are first to try your hands at reason.
If the Southern blood arises the speaker

signals and we begin 'the snaking out.'
Keep the slave hunter (SH) in center.

The committee speaker (S) stays in back.
(C) member takes hold of the hunter's head.

(A1 and A2) take hold of the arms.
(F1 and F2) take hold of the feet.

Pretending to try and rescue (SH)
12 more with oak billies loaded with lead

surround the group and rush to our carriage.
One plagued in this way will not invite others.

New England Emigrant Aid Company, 1854

Amos A. Lawrence, trustee, treasurer

To promote the emigration to Kansas Territory of persons opposed to slavery there, and to prevent by all means its establishment there.

To procure for these emigrants cheap fare, good accommodation, to advise them all through agents on their arrival out, in regard to eligible sites for settlements.

To secure for their benefit, by purchase or otherwise, advantageous locations as landing places, a general rendezvous for outfitting purposes.

To erect receiving houses for the temporary convenience for settlers' families.

To establish furnishing stores at which, on reasonably low terms, the necessities and comforts of life may be purchased.

To erect, or aid individuals in erecting and conducting saw-mills, grist mills, machine shops, and similar establishments essential in new settlements.

To introduce the printing press and thus afford a medium of communication between the settlers, their friends, and the public.

Lawrence, Kansas

Many of our people
are very much attached
to your name, Mr. Lawrence.

After I explained your course
in connection to this enterprise
and your characteristics

as they have been shown to me,
enthusiasm manifested.
It will be impossible

to induce our people to change
the name of their city
for any considerations.

We thought the one who stepped first
into the darkest of hours
of the grand enterprise

to urge on lagging energies
and move it with the firmest
'sinews of war' was worthy.

'Mid Western wilds
in freedom's cause
we'll make our happy home.

To make the West
as you the East
a homestead of the free!'

Figure 15. *Southern Chivalry*

Charles Sumner

1854

A god was challenged by a humble feat.
I bet you can't lift my cat off the ground.

The laughing god placed just one of his hands
under the belly of the little feline.

The god's face rained with sweat as he tried
but he could barely arch the cat's small back.

He saw that this was no ordinary cat.
This was the Serpent that coils Kansas!

Then Preston Brooks from South Carolina
all but caned me to death on the Senate floor!

Then one thousand men sacked Lawrence, Kansas;
called it a Boston Abolition Town.

Then John Brown's band of Free State Volunteers
hacked Doyle and Wilkinson, and shot Sherman.

Letter to Senator Atchinson

Amos A. Lawrence, 1855

We know you and your friends would make slave states.
We're working to prevent your doing so.

The ground has been chosen. Large are the stakes.
We shall fight. Let the fight be a fair one.

It is to secure this that I write you.
Your influence must restrain your people

from the injustices they are doing.
Use your efforts to avert this evil.

Your Missourians slip through the night
with revolvers and Bowie knives to vote.

They cast your votes and then go home.
The next morning they are nowhere in sight.

If you oppress us we bring our rifles.
We value rights more than you value life.

Letter to President Pierce

Amos A. Lawrence, July 15, 1855

It's evident that there is a body
of men in Missouri most determined

to drive our people from Kansas.
I must say that if they dare to do so

they will permanently suffer consequences.
You have a problem with the settlers

from the 'free States' opposed
to the introduction of the slave trade.

I note that you have now forced those settlers
to the conclusion that if they be safe

they must defend themselves out there.
I too have come to the same conclusion.

I have therefore rendered them assistance
by furnishing such means of defense.

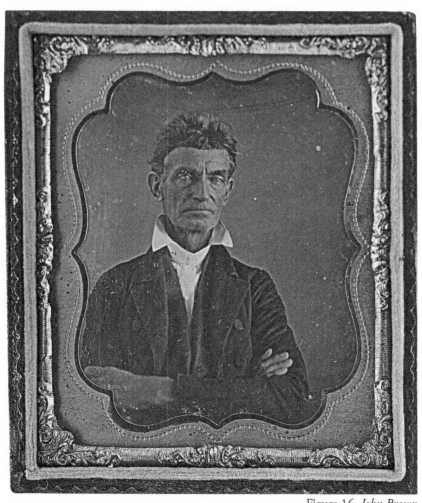

Figure 16. *John Brown*

Farmers Turned Soldiers

Amos A. Lawrence to Dr. Charles Robinson, 1855

When farmers turn soldiers they must have arms.
To fight for freedom you will need a gun.
Never again shall they burn down your barns.

To protect your freedom I send John Brown.
He has the look of a determined one.
When farmers turn soldiers they must have arms.

This is a simple case of right and wrong.
I send Sharps rifles so the ruffians run.
Never again shall they burn down your barns.

You must defend yourselves. Sound the alarms!
If they want to fight they will be outdone.
When farmers turn soldiers they must have arms.

You cannot afford your livelihood scarred.
Think of your wives, your daughters, your sons.
Never again shall they burn down your barns.

We have to appeal to the higher laws.
Everyone is equal under the sun.

When farmers turn soldiers they must be armed.
Never again shall they burn down your barns.

Figure 17. *John Brown Treason Broadside*

The Miles Standish of Kansas

Amos A. Lawrence, 1856 and 1859

Few people know of this man's character.
He is the last one to proclaim merit.

He's a true Puritanic warrior.
I esteem the loss of his services.

I bought wool from him back in '43.
I have known a lot more of him since then.

He has the look of a determined man.
Capitan John Brown is a Kansas hero.

He beat Missourians at Osawatomie.
At Pottawatomie and Harper's Ferry

he took the higher law much too far.
Regardless, he must be justly tried.

From his blood will spring an army of martyrs
all too eager to die for liberty.

EXPULSION OF NEGROES AND ABOLITIONISTS FROM TREMONT TEMPLE, BOSTON, MASSACHUSETTS, ON DECEMBER 3, 1860.—[SEE PAGE 787.]

Figure 18. *Expulsion of negroes and abolitionists from Tremont Temple, Boston, Massachusetts*

Commemoration of John Brown's Execution

Frederick Douglass, Tremont Temple, December 3, 1860

Nothing stands
where it stood yesterday.

This great city,
the Athens of America,

was convulsed by the rage
of a howling mob

sweeping onward
with silver hands

gleaning scattered ashes
in golden urns.

A thousand flowers
for a single fruit.

A thousand eggs
for a single fish or bird.

The mob blocked your streets,
shut up your halls,

and madly clamored
for the blood

of one whose name
adds lustre

to the very name of
Boston!

THE GALLANT CHARGE OF THE FIFTY FOURTH MASSACHUSETTS (COLORED) REGIMENT.
On the Rebel works at Fort Wagner, Morris Island near Charleston, July 18,th 1863, and death of Colonel Robt G. Shaw.

Figure 19. *The Gallant Charge of the 54th Mass. [colored] regiment of the rebel works of Ft. Wagner*

For the 54th Regiment

Amos A. Lawrence, May 28, 1863

I watched our Negroes march from Franklin Street.
Bands were playing, people cheering.

Governor Andrew asked me to recruit
this colored regiment of volunteers.

When Shaw came round he raised his hat to me.
He waved it to me twice, flags were flaunted.

These heroes march, determined in their youth.
All Boston turned out to watch them depart.

Would to God. Would to God. How I wish
I could fight the battles for these young men.

May God bless every one of these young souls.
May God save our country from all its foes.

May God crush rebellion with these Negroes,
and make Slavery a word no one knows.

The Last Full Measure of Devotion

My sword got stuck between his ribs.
I kicked my foot into his chest.
I pulled it out with both hands.

In the same motion I swung right
into the gut of another.
He hit the ground; I grabbed his Colt.

I shot one who was charging me
with a rifle and bayonet
soaked with blood and blue cloth.

'Without support of any kind'
Captain said 'retire by prolong'
so McGlivery could fill the gap.

We went quiet when he said
'Hold position at all hazards.'
I thrust my sword even harder

into a Mississippi thigh
as he tried to kick it from my hand
then go after our best gunner.

I used rammer heads. I used hand-spikes.
I kicked them in the groin.
I kneed them in the face.

Then I shot them in the stomach.
There was so much smoke around me
I didn't know their numbers.

Too many Barksdale sharpshooters.
Too many from South Carolina.
Too many 21st Mississippi.

Too many rocks for our wooden wheels.
Too many dying men and horses
to move our Napoleons back.

We saw Bigelow get shot twice
but the bugler took him to the rear.
We kept on trying to fight.

I got stabbed twice in the ankle.
I felt the shell go in my side.
My eyes were open when I died.

Notes

"Pirating the Power Loom" features **Francis Cabot Lowell** (1775–1817), co-founder of the Boston Manufacturing Company, writing to Nathan Appleton, his business partner. Lowell notoriously stole the plans for the power loom from Lancashire and brought them back to establish the first one-stop textile manufacturing facility in the world, in Waltham, Massachussets. The city of Lowell, Massachusetts, is named after him.

"Girl Power" refers to the fact that young women were the 'power' behind the power loom in the United States. Lowell and **Paul Moody** (1779–1831), the mechanic and inventor who partnered with Lowell, had a a grand plan. By hiring young girls from nearby farms they could absorb the surplus labor from the country, who would send money home to their father farmers, and have a more docile workforce that wouldn't strike as the Luddites had in Britain. Moody took Lowell's pirated designs, made America's first power loom and devised the 'Waltham-Lowell' system that went from 'bale to bolt,' where cotton bales went into the factory and full cloth came out.

"Tariff Act" of 1816 was a rare case of **Thomas Jefferson** supporting the Hamiltonian vision of raising tariffs on manufactured goods from the United States. With a high tariff on textiles from Britain the new mills in Massachusetts could corner the US and growing world markets. Jefferson had a more provincial, agrarian view of the U.S economy, but favored the act because it represented market opportunities for southern plantations.

"Removal Act" pays homage to the 'trail of tears' left by Native Americans who were forced to leave the southeastern United States in order to make room for the booming cotton slave plantations that sprang up as a result of the new demand for cotton.

"Lowell Cloth" is the name given by southerners to the cloth that clothed many of the slaves in southern cotton plantations. Cotton picked by slaves, made into shirts in Lowell, sold back to plantations to clothe slaves.

"**Lucy Larcom**" (1824–1893) was a poet, memoirst, former Lowell 'Mill Girl,' and later collaborator with John Greenleaf Whittier. 'tearless southern sky' is from Larcon's poem "Weaving."

"Athens of America": as noted by **Abbott Lawrence** (1792–1855), a businessman who with his brother Amos founded A. & A. Lawrence and Co., owner of Essex Company, A. & A. Lawrence and Co., congressman, ambassador. Co-founder of the city of Lawrence, Kansas, Robert Means was a wealthy southern planter. Topliffs was a famous sitting club for the Boston elite. Gottlieb Graupner (1767–1836) brought secular music to the United States. He had been in Haydn's orchestra; also noted for having started the minstrel 'negro song' movement in the north.

"Goodwill Tour": **Amos Lawrence** (1786–1852) textile businessman, owner of Essex Company, A. & A. Lawrence and Co., co-founder of the city of Lawrence, sends **Amos A. Lawrence** (1814–1886). Known as the 'Prince of the Cotton Whigs,' Amos A. Lawrence became a major textile businessman in his own right. He was a fervent defender of the constitution and states' rights. Lawrence was sent to the South by his father and uncle at an early age to solidify relationships with southern plantations and slaveholders. Rose to the heights of the Boston and national aristocracy. Became abolitionist after the passage of the Kansas-Nebraska Act and the case of Anthony Burns under the Fugitive Slave Act.

"Turnout" introduces **Harriet Hanson Robinson** (1825–1911), former Lowell 'Mill Girl,' poet, and woman's suffrage activist. She was a major part of the Lowell Strike or 'turnout,' where as many as 1500 women walked out of the mills demanding better pay and working conditions. Some Langston Hughes here, too.

"Warning Shots" is a note from **John Floyd** (1783–1837), Governor of Virginia. Incensed from Nat Turner's revolt, he fires off letters to Boston's elite warning them to uphold the alliance.

"Letter of Reassurance" is from **Harrison Gray Otis** (1765–1848), Boston businessman, Mayor at the time, and later United States Senator.

"*The Liberator*" refers to **William Lloyd Garrison** (1805–1879), famous Boston abolitionist and publisher of *The Liberator*.

"This is No Party" evokes speeches by **Wendell Phillips** (1811–1884), Boston orator and lawyer, who leaves Whig party to become abolitionist.

Known as a 'conscience whig' rather than a 'cotton whig.'

"*The Boston Whig*" refers to the newspaper of the same name that represented the Whig party in Massachusetts.

The "Compromise of 1850" gave rise to the Fugitive Slave Act and designated new territories to be a mix of free and slave states.

"**Thomas Sims**" (1834–?), was an enslaved African-American slave who escaped from Georgia to Boston but was convicted under the Fugitive Slave Act.

"**Anthony Burns**" (1834–1862), Alexandria, Virginia, born slave who escapes to Massachusetts but is convicted under the Fugitive Slave Act and is returned to his master.

"Rescue Attempt": **Thomas Wentworth Higginson** was a Unitarian minister and member of the Boston Vigilance committee that led an attack on the court house to try and rescue Anthony Burns. Higginson was also a member of the secret six that supported John Brown.

"Skunk Peculiarities" features **Richard Henry Dana** (1815–1882), defense lawyer for Anthony Burns.

"The Foot of Slave Power" is **Samuel May, Jr.** (1810–1899), citizen of Boston, member of Massachusetts Anti-Slavery Society's reflection on the escort of Anthony Burns back to slavery.

"Boston Anti-Man-Hunting League" reveals the secret formation of the league as laid out by **Henry Bowditch** (1808–1892), prominent Boston physician and abolitionist. With many of the Boston elite, including Amos A. Lawrence, formed and funded the secret Boston Anti-Man Hunting League after the Anthony Burns trial. Eli Thayer (1819–1899), instigator of "Kansas Crusade."

"Lawrence, Kansas" notes the founding of that town, named after Amos A. Lawrence. The last two stanzas are from **John Greenleaf Whittier**'s commemorative poem to those from Massachusetts who emigrated to Kansas to help make it a free state.

"Charles Sumner" (January 6, 1811–March 11, 1874), Massachusetts Senator who coined the term 'unholy alliance' between the 'lords of the lash' and the 'lords of the loom.' Sumner denounced the Kansas-Nebraska Act on the Senate floor and was severely beaten by South Carolina Senator Preston Brooks. Amos A. Lawrence accommodated Sumner's recovery.

"Letter to Senator Atchinson" is addressed to **David Rice Atchinson** (1807–1886); Senator from Missouri. Lawrence wrote to draw a line in the sand, and later to **Dr. Charles Robinson** (1818–1894), first Governor of Kansas, to tell him he would support Kansas' bid to be a free state.

"Miles Standish of Kansas" refers to John Brown (May 9, 1800–December 2, 1859), who with the support of Amos A. Lawrence Brown led the effort to make Kansas a free state, well before Harper's Ferry.

"Commemoration of John Brown's Execution" depicts **Frederick Douglass** (1818–1895), leader, reformer, former slave, abolitionist, diplomat. Garrison and Douglass were thrown out of Tremont Temple, the Jewish temple where a commemoration was held for John Brown's hanging.

"For the **54ᵗʰ Regiment**," one of the first African American units in the Civil War. Amos A. Lawrence was a core recruiter and financier of the unit.

Artwork

The illustrations appear in the following order. All are in the public domain; thanks to the sources given:

Figure 1. Baines, Edward, *Power loom weaving. History of the cotton manufacture.* Published by Edward Baines, 1835.

Figure 2. Frost, John, *Pictorial Life of Andrew Jackson*, Hartford, Belknap and Hamersley, Philadelphia, M. Bomberger (etc., etc.), 1840. Washington, Library of Congress.

Figure 3. Johnston, David Claypoole, 1799–1865, *The House that Jack Built: Boston.* Drawn and published by David Claypool Johnston, 1863, etching on wove paper; 27.5 x 36.7 cm. Washington, Library of Congress.

Figure 4. Homer, Winslow, *New England Factory Life.* July 26, 1868, 9 ¼ x 14 in. (23.5 x 35.6 cm). Smithsonian American Art Museum.

Figure 5. Gleason's; *S. Klous & Co. Hat, Cap, and Fur Store, Court Street, Boston*, 1852, Gleason's Pictorial, Courtesy of the Trustees of the Boston Public Library/Rare Books.

Figure 6. Dennis, Robert N., Stereoscopic views of Faneuil Hall, Quincy and Washington Markets, Boston, Massachusetts; New York Public Library, Digital Collection.

Figure 7. *Ladies Department, The Liberator,* William Lloyd Garrison, editor, New England Historical Society.

Figure 8. Masthead, *The Liberator*, edited by William Lloyd Garrison, Boston, 1831, designed by Hammatt Billings, Boston Athenaeum.

Figure 9. Parker, Theodore, 1810–1860, "First anniversary of the kidnapping of Thomas Sims by the City of Boston" broadside. Boston Public Library, Rare Books & Manuscripts Department.

Figure 10. *Portrait of Anthony Burns*, R.M. Edwards, printer, 129 Congress Street, Boston, c. 1855. Washington, Library of Congress.

Figure 11. *Night Attack on the Court House*, Charles Emery Stevens, Anthony Burns: A History, 1856. Washington, Library of Congress.

Figure 12. Andrews, E. Benjamin, "The rendition of Anthony Burns in Boston." History of the United States from the Earliest Discovery of America to the Present Day, Volume III (New York: Charles Scribner's Sons, 1895).

Figure 13. Drawing of Amos Adams Lawrence, the founder of Lawrence University. This image appears in the margin of a map of the city of Appleton, 1859. Lawrence University Archives.

Figure 14. Bowditch, Henry I., 1854–1859, "Diagram to show the drill the Anti-Man-Hunting League had for the running off of a slave- or man-hunter," Reprinted with permission of the Massachusetts Historical Society.

Figure 15. Magee, John L. (c.1820–c.1870), *Southern Chivalry—Argument versus Club's*, 1856. Reprinted with permission of the Boston Athenaeum.

Figure 16. Bowles, John (1833–1900), *John Brown*, circa 1856. Reprinted with permission of the Boston Athenaeum.

Figure 17. *John Brown Treason Broadside*. Executive Papers of Governor Henry A. Wise, 1856–1859. Accession 36710. State Government Records Collection, The Library of Virginia, Richmond, Virginia.

Figure 18. Homer, Winslow, *Expulsion of negroes and abolitionists from Tremont Temple, Boston, Massachusetts, on December 3, 1860*, Published in *Harper's Weekly*, 15 December 1860, p. 788. Winslow Homer Collection, Boston Public Library, Print Department.

Figure 19. *The Gallant Charge of the 54th Mass. [colored] regiment of the rebel works of Ft. Wagner ... July 18, 1863*. Currier and Ives, 1863. *African-American Perspectives: The Progress of a People*, Library of Congress.

Sources

This book is derived, adapted from, and inspired by the following diaries, correspondences, speeches, books, and scholarly works:

Appleton, Nathan (1856), *Memoir of Hon. Abbott Lawrence*, Boston: J. Eastman.

Appleton, Nathan (1858), *Introduction to the Power Loom and the Founding of Lowell*, Lowell: P.H. Penhallow.

Blatt, Martin and David Roediger (1999), *The Meaning of Slavery in the North*, New York and London: Garland Publishing.

Bowditch, Vincent (1902), *The Life and Correspondence of Henry Bowditch*, Boston: Houghton Mifflin.

Brauer, Kinley (1967), *Cotton Versus Conscience: Massachusetts Whig Politics and Southwestern Expansion 1843-1848*, Lexington: University of Kentucky Press.

Broyles, Michael, "Music and Class Structure in Antebellum Boston," *Journal of the American Musicological Society*, V, 44, N. 3 (Autumn, 1991),451-493.

Bullins, Ed (1969), *Five Plays*, New York: Bobbs-Merrill.

Dalzell, Robert (1987), *Enterprising Elite: The Boston Associates and the World They Made*, Cambridge: Harvard University Press.

Garrison, William Lloyd (1852), *Selections from the Writings and Speeches of William Lloyd Garrison*, Boston: R.F. Wallcut.

Goodman, Paul, "The Values of a Boston Elite, 1800–1860," *American Quarterly*, Vol. 18, No. 3 (Autumn, 1966), pp. 437-456.

Heaney, Seamus (1976), *North*, Faber, Oxford University Press, New York, NY.

Larcom, Lucy (1875), *The Idyl of Work*, Boston: James R. Osgood.

Lawrence, Amos (1855), *Extracts from the Diary and Correspondence of Amos Lawrence*, Boston: Hobart.

Lawrence, William (1899), *Life of Amos A. Lawrence*, Boston: Houghton and Mifflin and Company.

O'Connor, Thomas (1968), *Lords of the Loom: The Cotton Whigs and the Coming of the Civil War*, New York: Scribner's Sons.

Olmstead, Frederic Law Omsted (1996), *The Cotton Kingdom: A Traveller's Observations on Cotton and Slavery in the American Slave States, 1853–1861*, De Capo Press.

Olson, Charles (1960), *The Maximus Poems*, George Butterick (ed), University of California Press.

Robinson, Harriet Hanson (1898), *Loom and Spindle*, New York: T.R. Crowell.

Rosenberg, Chaim (2011), *The Life and Times of Francis Cabot Lowell*, San Francisco, Rowman and Littlefield.

Rukeyser, Muriel (1938), *U.S. 1*, New York, Covici, Friede.

Stauffer, John, Zoe Trodd, Celeste-Marie Bernier (2015), *Picturing Frederick Douglass*, New York, Liverright Books.

Stevens, Charles Emergy (1856), *Anthony Burns: A History*, Boston: John P. Jewett.

United States Work Progress Administration, Federal Writers Project, Manuscript Division, Library of Congress, South Carolina Narratives, Part 4, Rosa Starke.

Von Frank, Albert (1998), *The Trials of Anthony Burns*, Cambridge: Harvard University Press.

Wheelwright, John Brooks (1938), *Mirrors of Venus: A Novel in Sonnets*, Boston: Bruce Humphries.

Whittier, John Greenleaf (1877), *Complete Poetical Works of John Greenleaf Whittier*, Boston: John R. Osgood.

Williams, William Carlos (1963) *Paterson*, New York: New Directions.

About the Author

KEVIN GALLAGHER is a political economist, poet and publisher living in Greater Boston with his wife Kelly, their children Theo and Estelle, and Rexroth, the family's German shepherd. Gallagher edits *spoKe*, a Boston-based annual of poetry and poetics, and works as a Professor of Global Development Policy at Boston University's Pardee School for Global Studies.